Fraser in Office

Denis White

Foreword By David Kemp

Jeparit Press

Published in 2022 by Connor Court Publishing Pty Ltd under the Jeparit Press Imprint

Jeparit Press is an imprint of Connor Court Publishing in conjunction with the Menzies Research Centre.

Menzies Research Centre
R.G. Menzies House
1 Macquarie St
Barton
ACT 2600
www.menziesrc.org

Copyright © 2022, Denis White

All rights reserved. No part of this book may be reproduced or transmitted in any form or by any means, electronic or mechanical, including photo copying, recording or by any information storage and retrieval system, without prior permission in writing from the publisher.

Connor Court Publishing Pty Ltd
PO Box 7257
Redland Bay QLD 4165
sales@connorcourt.com
www.connorcourt.com
Phone 0497-900-685

Printed in Australia

ISBN: 978-1-922449-58-0

Front cover design: Branded Graphics

Dedicated to the Memory of my Parents

Kenneth Francis White and Audrey Margaret White (nee Atkinson)

Table of Contents

Intorduction Note by Nick Cater	7
Foreword by David Kemp	9
Acknowledgements	21
Malcolm Fraser in Government	25
- Overview	27
- Politics	28
- Liberalism	30
- Leadership	36
- Opposition	37
- Government	47
- Taxing and Spending	52
- Deregulation	55
- Human Dignity, the Constitution, and The Environment	57
- International	60
- Moving On	64
Malcolm Fraser Quotations	65
Malcolm Fraser Timeline	79
Select Bibliography	95

Introduction Note by Nick Cater

Malcolm Fraser served as Prime Minister of Australia for seven years and 122 days, ranking him third in the pantheon of Liberal leaders in government, and the fourth longest serving prime minister of any political party. It was a prime ministership of substance. At the start of Fraser's first term, the nation was deeply divided over the misjudgements of an impetuous, ideologically driven leader and the manner of his departure. Fraser relinquished the prime ministership in more conventional circumstances having set the stage for 23 years of stable, reforming government by a largely centrist Labor administration and a Liberal-led Coalition that governed firmly in the national interest.

Fraser's part in restoring order to government and reviving the fortunes of liberalism has received far less attention than it deserves. The events that preceded his appointment and controversies in his retirement have compromised the assessment of his legacy by obscuring its undoubted achievements. Six years after Fraser's death, a fresh appraisal is overdue, one unclouded by the political arguments in his post-parliamentary years or the extraordinary dismissal of his predecessor by the governor-general. It is time for a discussion unsullied by the wisdom of hindsight, that calibrates his achievements according to the condition of the country he inherited and the one he left behind.

Denis White's monograph is intended to start a conversation

that is long overdue. Our hope is that it will broaden our perspective not just on Fraser, but on the purpose of the Liberal Party and how it can better serve the people it wishes to govern. If the Howard government showed us how to manage a good economy, the Fraser government helps us understand why we should, since Liberalism, as Robert Menzies conceived it, regards economic prosperity as the means to a greater end. A strong economy was the foundation on which to build a country that is just and fair, in which the provision of material needs goes hand in hand with enhancing human dignity.

The monograph will have served its purpose if it deepens appreciation of Fraser's legacy, and broadens our understanding of what the Liberal Party should aspire to be.

Nick Cater

Executive Director, Menzies Research Centre

January 2022

Foreword by David Kemp

Few people worked as closely with Malcolm Fraser, or knew him better, than Dr. Denis White. White had a rare insight into Fraser's mind as a speech writer and adviser over many years. His intimate knowledge of, and respect for, Fraser's thinking, and thought processes, is reflected in this unique and important, albeit too brief, account of one of Australia's longest serving prime ministers.

Denis White was Director of the Prime Minister's Office in 1982-3; commencing in the Office after the 1980 election. After Fraser left parliamentary politics he sought Denis' advice on speeches and papers, and on the development of his 2002 collection of speeches *Common Ground*. When Fraser left parliament, Denis and I edited a small book of Fraser's views and reflections on many matters with which he had dealt as prime minister (D.M. White, D.A. Kemp, *Malcolm Fraser on Australia, Melbourne, Hill of Content, 1986*). Denis arranged for a foreword by the American former Secretary of State, Dr. Henry Kissinger, who wrote of his respect for Fraser as an 'uncommonly interesting man and thinker'.

'Malcolm Fraser in Government' was originally written in 2001 as a contribution to a book of essays on Liberal Party history, but not published at the time because of editorial differences. It was thus composed when Fraser was still alive, and has a vividness in its personal observations that reflect this. The changes to it in this version are minor, but helpful for the current reader, and with additions to one or two points. The text remains a key document for understanding Fraser and his legacy as prime minister as perceived by one of his closest advisers.

Malcolm Fraser has a very important place in the story of Australian liberalism. He provides a vital link to, and development of, the liberalism of Robert Menzies, especially in relation to the continuing policy significance of the central emphasis of Menzies' liberalism on the importance of the freedom and dignity of the individual person. Fraser was self-consciously in the Menzies tradition, and justifiably saw himself as pursuing reform based on Menzies' central value as he sought to strengthen the rights and capacities of individual people to take control of their own lives, to choose, and to exercise their democratic rights. He was less conservative than Menzies in relation to reform of the liberal institutions of government, seeing the need for further mechanisms to succeed in the fight against prejudice and to empower individuals to assert their democratic rights in relation to a state that had exploded in size under Whitlam. White's essay provides a highly informed perspective on why and how he went about this.

White is an accomplished strategic thinker, and in this paper he is conscious of the major tasks Fraser faced as a decision-maker and as an advocate on national issues. These, he tells us, included the importance of facts, of direction, of crystallizing issues, of size and scale. He shows how Fraser sought to apply his liberal philosophy to policy, and highlights the influence a liberal leader could have in shaping the public agenda. White's paper reminds us, as he wrote in another context, of the 'toughness of politics', and of what 'running the country' was like.

Denis White was in many respects a unique 'fit' with Fraser, because Fraser was a man who took ideas seriously, and White was by profession a political philosopher, who had taught the subject at Monash University, and had published professional papers on such topics as 'Constitutionalism', 'Power and Liberty', and the 'Study of Democracy'. White had long been interested in the intersection of philosophy and practical politics. Before accepting an appointment in Fraser's office, he had written a book on *The Philosophy of the Australian Liberal Party*[1], and a further philosophical work, *The World of Man*, which embodied his understanding of the meaning of life and the world mankind inhabits.[2]

Fraser was a prime minister with an explicit interest in political ideas and in liberal thought and principles, and his understanding of these ideas, and the idealism derived from them, undoubtedly influenced his policy priorities and the directions of policy he pursued. They later became the weapons he deployed in debate with the Liberal governments that followed. Where Menzies' liberalism owed a heavy debt to his legal education, Fraser's studies in PPE at Oxford had introduced him to the leading political philosophers, Hobbes, Machiavelli, Locke, Mill and others. Denis White points out that Fraser had concluded from these studies that it fell to the elected politician to find the best answers to practical problems through applying liberal ideas to achieve humane and democratic policies.

---

1 *The Philosophy of the Australian Liberal Party*, (Melbourne, Hutchinson, 1978).
2 *The World of Man*, (South Carolina, The Create Space Independent Publishing Platform, 2013).

Ideas were important to Fraser. He enjoyed debating ideas and attempting to apply them to policy. His speeches before and after becoming prime minister are replete with his analysis of the values and principles on which he believed policy should be based. He surrounded himself with advisers whom, he thought, could help him clarify his thinking, and communicate it to the public service and the electorate, on the many difficult issues a prime minister faces.

His senior office staff during his term as prime minister had comprised advisers with established academic reputations or promise, with whom he enjoyed and sought discussions on the ideas that should guide policy decisions, and on policy itself. These included the economists Prof. John Rose and Prof. Cliff Walsh, a later famous radio talk-show host, Alan Jones, and political scientists such as myself, Petro Georgiou and the philosopher, Denis White. Owen Harries, a foreign affairs specialist attached to Foreign Minister Andrew Peacock, also was drawn into his intellectual circle, as were some of the most creative policy minds in his own and other departments, such as Ian Castles (Treasury and Finance), Ed Visbord, Michael Keating (Prime Minister and Cabinet), Fred Wheeler, John Stone (Treasury), and Harry Knight (Reserve Bank).

Despite all the intellectual fire-power he gathered around him, when all is said and done, it is plausible that what distinguished Fraser's thinking about politics was its continuity. In relation to budgetary policy and economic management his liberalism was that of Robert Menzies: believing in private enterprise and reward for effort as the sources of opportunity and prosperity, with government as the guardian of the public interest. Like Menzies, he believed in limited government, and—challenged by the explosion of government spending and centralized regulation of the Whitlam government—foreshadowed Thatcher and Reagan in his opposition to 'big' government (as both these other leaders recognized).

Circumstances, however, had changed since Menzies. The Arbitration Commission, under pressure from a reinvigorated union leadership, after the O'Shea case of 1969, had strengthened the industrial power of the unions and adopted a policy of indexing wages to inflation. The Fraser government found itself coping with the consequences of the first oil shock, and an economy destabilized by wage increases far beyond productivity, substantial industrial unrest, and a protected industry sector reeling from Whitlam's 25 per cent tariff cut. The fixed exchange rate had produced a significantly overvalued dollar. Fraser was deeply troubled by the impact on families, the human cost, and the loss of confidence, that economic destablisation had imposed, and he unceasingly sought the instruments at his disposal—budgetary, institutional and industrial—to return to stability.

Through will-power and strength of character Fraser successfully reined in government spending, instituted flexible management of the exchange rate, insisted on a more independent policy voice for the Reserve Bank, legislatively curtailed some excesses of union power, and attempted reform of the Arbitration Commission with the same objective. He did not support further reductions in tariffs under the circumstances he faced, fearing further short-term collapse in the protected industries. He used fiscal policy, regulation and industrial bargaining to haul back Whitlam's 'wage overhang', but the second oil shock of 1979, and the wage explosion of 1981, revealed the bankruptcy of the traditional economic policy framework and the limits of the policy instruments on which government had traditionally relied.

It must be noted that there was no significant voice in Australia calling for substantial deregulation of the labour market during Fraser's time as prime minister, so he never considered this policy direction. He suspected also that the rising voices of the freer market 'dries' in his last term after 1980, calling for a more open deregulated economy, were seeking resurrection of a selfish 'laissez faire' of the kind Menzies had disowned.

In retrospect, Fraser himself conceded that he wished he had been able to do more on labour market reform, and that in economic policy his government was to some extent, 'transitional'. While economic liberalism acquired new understandings and strategies during the Fraser years, his loyalty to the Menzies economic policy heritage, in very difficult domestic and international circumstances, let him down, as an empowered union movement in 1980-81 took control of the wages policy agenda, once more lifting inflation and unemployment, and costing him office at the 1983 election.

Fraser was also a believer in the devolution of governmental power in Australia, and he came to office in 1975 with what some in the press described as a 'revolutionary' New Federalism policy, designed to counter Labor's passion for centralization with newly empowered and properly accountable state governments. Fraser was strongly opposed to Whitlam's undermining of the states by centralizing policy control in Canberra. The Liberal Party had been rewarded at the 1975 election by winning every seat but one in Queensland (Oxley), every seat but one in Western Australia (Fremantle), and every seat in Tasmania, reducing Labor to an urban rump. His New Federalism was the centerpiece of his answer to Whitlam's centralization of power. It was a bold policy to enable the states in effect to levy income tax through a surcharge to be collected by the Commonwealth, but distributed according to rates set by them. It was radical and innovative, and largely the product of John Carrick, but no state took advantage of it, and it was an initiative still-born. The states preferred lack of responsibility to strengthening their financial base.

Fraser's liberalism, as had Menzies', centred on his belief in human dignity, and the freedom and equality of all people and peoples. Fraser was an activist, and this value informed, not only his attitudes to government and his economic policies, but his education policies, his policies for aboriginal people, migrants, refugees, and the Third World of developing countries.

He was, as White says, a committed democrat in his attitudes to people. Add to this the moral obligation he felt to the people of South Vietnam arising from Australia's participation in the failed American adventure, and it should have been no surprise that from 1976 he welcomed Vietnamese refugees coming by boat, and that his government eventually sought out in refugee camps, some 70,000 refugees from the conflict in southeast Asia. The personal satisfaction and pride he felt in having carried out this humane policy, to Australia's great advantage, he believed, was at the root of his later alienation from the policies towards boat people by the Keating and Howard governments. He did not concede, as these later governments argued, that the greater numbers arriving by boat, and the role of people smuggling, was a justification for the change in national policy. Many disagreed.

In retrospect, it seems clear that Fraser's most important

policy achievements and legacies are the product of his focus on liberalism's core belief in equal human dignity. He was shocked by Whitlam's de jure recognition of Soviet occupation of the Baltic States, and disgusted by the inhumanity of communism. Nevertheless, all Australian governments owe debts to liberal thought, and Fraser was willing to bring to fruition unfulfilled liberal initiatives of the Whitlam government with which he agreed on moral and principled grounds in relation to Aboriginal land rights and basic human rights.

Fraser believed that Australia as an open liberal society had 'enormous capacity for social change' (Fraser, Simon, 427). His policies to acknowledge and strengthen the rights of Aboriginal people, and oppose prejudice, are widely acknowledged. Charles Perkins, former Aboriginal activist, a leader who had held senior public service office under both Whitlam and Fraser, said of the latter's conduct of Aboriginal affairs that Fraser 'was absolutely A-1. He was tops, he was the best of them all on Aboriginal affairs. And Gough is good, but you know the problem with Gough … sometimes he thinks he started everything … and he didn't'. (Fraser, Simon, 401).

Fraser was not a 'do-gooder'. He brought a strong sense of morality and concern for others to policy, and while giving way to moralism from time to time, constantly sought to align policy and values. His moral opposition to racism informed both his domestic and foreign policies, from his early enactment of inalienable title to land for aboriginal communities in the Northern Territory (1976) through to his pursuit of a unifying strategy with African nations in the Commonwealth Heads of Government forum. As prime minister, and after he left office, he was a resolute opponent of apartheid in South Africa. His establishment of the Australian Human Rights Commission in 1981 was prompted principally by his concern with prejudice against Aboriginal people.

In pursuit of his mission, Fraser was prepared to take on those on his own side of politics, in the states and in his own federal parliamentary party, who were more conservative than he was on such matters. Premiers Joh Bjelke-Petersen in Queensland, Charles Court in Western Australia, and Robin Gray in Tasmania, would become critics in the face of Fraser's defence of human values, or of parts of Australia's natural environment of world heritage quality such as Fraser Island, the Great Barrier Reef, or the Tasmanian Lake Pedder, against development projects, where he saw more fundamental principles or values at stake.

The Premiers described this as centralism, but Fraser, though prepared to use Commonwealth power, was not a centralist, and would, as in the Tasmanian Dams case episode, and in other instances, acknowledge and support the Federal division of powers at considerable political cost to himself. Nevertheless, like all federal Liberal Party leaders, he experienced the policy tension arising from the gift, conferred on the Commonwealth by the Constitution, of governmental power grounded in financial strength and over-riding legislative authority. He used this gift powerfully, and controversially, from time to time to protect what he saw as crucial human and other values.

Fraser's concern with individual rights and the application of the rule of law was also expressed in the appointment of the first ombudsman in Australia in 1977, and the establishment of the Administrative Appeals Tribunal, empowered through the Administrative Decisions (Judicial review) Act in 1980. National freedom of information laws were passed in December 1982. Each of these reforms was a significant and lasting step in the continuing campaign to empower the citizen in relation to government, and to strengthen the democratic accountability of government officials.

One of Fraser's most memorable policy achievements was his policy to bring immigrants and their communities into a fuller participation in national life through recognition and respect. Some have argued that his policy of 'multiculturalism' contained the danger of tribalising Australia and diminishing national unity, and it is true that some attempted to take advantage of immigrant communities and their organisations for selfish political purposes, but national unity was always explicitly Fraser's objective. He saw the need, if unity were to be achieved, to construct institutions that would reassure migrants that they did not have to abandon their previous identity and their cultural heritage to be full members of the Australian community. It was a principle equally applicable to Aboriginal affairs. He believed that a modern Australian identity could include identities based on the recognition of diverse heritages, as it had with Scots and Irish. Programs to teach the English language and Australian democratic norms, alongside the Special Broadcasting Service and the Institute for Multicultural Affairs, were lasting legacies of his policy, and underpin Australia's remarkable success as an immigrant nation.

In foreign affairs Fraser kept Australia's security at the front of his mind. With the Soviet Union still expansionary and eyeing opportunities in the Pacific, Fraser worked effectively to bring balance through the United States, Japan and China.

He saw the danger of America, after its experience in Vietnam, retreating from international leadership, and worked to prevent this through Australian support.

For Fraser, as White reminds us, 'life wasn't meant to be easy', and he worked idealistically and ceaselessly to resolve the dilemmas, and surmount the obstacles, that life placed in his way to achieve a better, freer, world.

David Kemp

January 2022

Acknowledgements

This sketch of Malcolm Fraser was written to do him justice. My hope is that it will help readers to perceive his measure as a thinker and a statesman. Fraser himself told me that he liked what I had written: being the man he was, he would not have said this if he had not thought it. It is fitting that the Menzies Research Centre is now publishing the work, and my thanks go to Nick Cater and the team.

As a sketch rather than a portrait— and a brief one at that — the challenge for the author was to capture the essence and essentials of Fraser and his three Governments. In substance, this has meant overviewing and exemplifying the character and power of Fraser's thinking, the strength of his will, his belief in 'a fair go', and his capacity to get things done.

The works cited in footnotes and the bibliography provide most of the relevant factual information, and the text also draws on my own experiences as a speechwriter in 1981, as Director of Fraser's Private Office in 1982-83, and as a friend who discussed and commented on many of his speeches, articles, books and general activities over the next 30-plus years.

Through all these years, whenever the phone rang at 7.30 in the morning, I always knew it would be Malcolm—who else would ring so early — and I often tried to guess what he would be ringing about. Not once did I guess right, for he was always out in front.

He was usually looking for a comment on his own fresh line of political reasoning that would become the next day's headline.

It is a privilege to be able to thank Fraser in print for all that he did for Australia and its people—especially those who worked for him. His high standards are of course legendary, and will long remain the Australian benchmark. He brought out the best in people—especially those who worked for him—by understanding them as individuals, respecting them as people, and requiring them to do their best. When a young acquaintance recently asked the most valuable thing I learned while working for Fraser, I surprised myself by saying that the most valuable thing I learned was how things are done at the highest level. For that, and much else, I will always be supremely grateful to this towering figure. As Prime Minister, he let nothing and nobody stand in the way of his responsibility and commitment to doing the best for Australia.

I am grateful to Nick Cater, not only for his decision that the Menzies Research Centre should publish these thoughts about Fraser, and not only for his suggestion to include the timeline, but also for his advice, enthusiasm and encouragement.

I feel honoured that The Menzies Research Centre is publishing this work. Menzies meant so much to Australia as a nation, and to countless individual Australians. I trust a personal reminiscence is permissible.

In 1968, having completed a wonderful university education that was made possible by three of the Commonwealth Scholarships for which Menzies was responsible, I sent him a letter of appreciation. I said that while it was hard to say what these scholarships had meant to me, they had meant virtually everything. I received a beautifully typed and personally signed letter, in which he thanked me for mine, and added:

> I receive very few letters of thanks for what I was able to do in the matter of education. Your letter is therefore the more appreciated.

I subsequently shook his hand at the graduation ceremony. He said of my thesis—titled *Moral Responsibility*—that it was a 'good topic'. But what really moved me on that occasion—Menzies was presiding as Chancellor of The University of Melbourne—was his kindness to the graduand ahead of me in the line. This man's face was affected by a medical condition, and being close to him I could not but realise that he was feeling awkward as he approached Menzies. Menzies, on turning towards him, immediately saw the man's discomfort. Without missing a beat, Menzies softly said a few words (I could not hear what) that immediately put the man at his ease and made him smile. Here was an unforgettable experience of the personal concern for others of a very great man.

I particularly thank David Kemp for his invaluable Foreword, and for his constant encouragement to keep working at ideas. For close to fifty years, David has been lighting the way for the Liberal Party. How we all owe him! In the context of this work, it is right that it be said that nobody did more for Fraser or gave more than David Kemp.

Above all, I thank my wife Carnie not only for her daily support and encouragement, but also for her unfailing awareness and commitment to the things that matter.

Malcolm Fraser in Government

Overview

Malcolm Fraser dominated Australian politics from 1975 to the 1983 election. He won three elections. He initiated a large turnaround in Australian life, through emphasizing government restraint, reduction and responsibility - while at the same time persuading Australians not to expect too much from government. He held the size of government relative to GDP. He advanced landmark initiatives in social and community reform, including Aboriginal rights, multiculturalism, family allowances, and the environment. He leveraged Australia's international influence in the traditional power centres of Europe and America, in the rapidly rising Asia-Pacific context, and in Africa. He demonstrated Australia's independence and moral convictions, most notably through his opposition to racism in southern Africa. This account explains these pre-occupations and achievements.

Fraser stands out as a remarkable national and international figure. Dr Henry Kissinger, one of the great diplomats of the era, said that he "found Malcolm Fraser, both in and out of office, an uncommonly interesting man and thinker".[3]

Fraser's road was not easy, and his way was not silky. In Australia, his reputation as Prime Minister has had a rocky path in some quarters, not least in his own party. The core criticism has two main strands: first, that he did not go far enough in reducing government; second, that he missed an opportunity to free up the economy. The first strand raises issues of judgment about how much would have been too much. The wisdom of hindsight comes into play. Fraser himself made statements which suggest he had

---

[3] See Kissinger's Foreword to *Malcolm Fraser on Australia*, ed. D M White and D A Kemp, Hill of Content, Australia, 1986, p. xv.

some sympathy with this criticism.[4] Some relevant factors are examined later in this work.

The second strand of criticism involves major and genuine policy differences both within and across political parties and commentators in Australia. These differences relate to a variety of issues, including government support of Australian firms and industries, micro-economic reform, the relationship of economic efficiency to other values, relationships between Australia and its trading partners. Fraser himself remained an active contributor to some of these debates for the rest of his life. In the year 2001 for example—six years before the Global Financial Crisis—he made a Centenary of Federation speech in which he commented, on the one hand that parties across the political spectrum have "all accepted the downsizing of government", and on the other that in the global environment, where the market can be "capricious, irrational, even fanciful,... there are two main tasks: How to establish stability within the financial markets themselves and how to preserve some form of equity and reasonable competition in a globalised market place".

Politics

Fraser made politics and policy his lifelong vocation. He was preselected for the federal seat of Wannon in 1953 when he was only twenty three years old—though he did not win that election. He became a Member of Parliament in the 1955 election, six years into Robert Menzies' record term. There is no doubt that Fraser

---

4 See Philip Ayres, *Malcolm Fraser A Biography*, Heinemann, Richmond, 1987, Chapter 14 and passim.

was greatly influenced by Menzies in his ways of thinking and acting in politics and government.[5] He became Minister for the Army in 1966 under Harold Holt. He subsequently became Minister for Education and Science (1968-69, and 1971-72), and Minister for Defence (1969-71). He resigned as Minister for Defence in 1971, in circumstances which led to the replacement of John Gorton by William McMahon as Prime Minister.[6]

Malcolm Fraser became Australia's youngest Prime Minister in 1975, when he was only 45 years old. He held office for more than seven years, and became Australia's second longest serving Prime Minister at that time. When he lost the 1983 election, and subsequently left the Parliament, he was still only 52 years old. Bob Hawke, the incoming Prime Minister, may have seemed the face of a newer age, but he was an older man than Fraser.

Because so many years have passed, this account of Malcolm Fraser in Government is primarily written for generations of Australians who have little or no memory of the Fraser years. It therefore focuses on enduring features of what Fraser did, on the directions in which he led Australia, on the circumstances in which he found himself, and on the philosophical perspective and other relevant qualities which he brought to the Prime Ministerial office.

---

[5] Sir John Bunting, Secretary of the Department of Prime Minister and Cabinet at that time, once told me that early in Fraser's Parliamentary career, Menzies asked him to make a point of introducing Fraser widely to people employed in the Public Service, because Fraser would become an important figure in Government and would need to know his way around the Public Service. When preparing speeches for Fraser in 1981, I was often amazed at the breadth and depth of his knowledge of capable and dedicated public servants, and his capacity to draw on their expertise. What a dividend for Menzies' perceptiveness!

[6] See Ayres, Op Cit, pp. 181-85.

Liberalism

Fraser's liberalism embraced a belief in the individual, and a cluster of surrounding values: freedom, democracy, human rights and dignity, the rule of law, parliamentary government, equality before the law, equality of opportunity, and an open, egalitarian Australia. In the context of economic policy, his belief in the individual led him to support private enterprise, particularly against various forms of monopoly. On the political front, he was passionately democratic. He was repulsed by unelected government. He was strongly committed to high standards in government, and thought it important not only what governments did, but how they did things. He was not a doctrinaire Liberal, but was profoundly resistant to the erosion of rights and liberties, and supportive of pragmatic measures to give people a "fair go".

Fraser had a clear, if complex view of the underlying nature of politics. His view was that politics is partly reactive and partly proactive. On the one hand, national life is made up of challenges and responses. From this perspective, governments must make hard decisions, and a good many of them. On the other hand, people and nations can carve out opportunities for themselves through politics, and thereby forge their own futures.

He believed in free will, and the acceptance of responsibility that goes with it. He did not believe that human history is inevitable—on the contrary, he had a strong sense of personal responsibility for creating outcomes. His views were partly based on his observation while studying great thinkers when he was at Oxford that while each of them explained part of reality, none of them—individually or collectively—succeeded in explaining everything.

In this sense, and partly for these reasons, he saw politics as the great profession. This was one of Fraser's major reasons for entering politics.[7] He believed that while there are limits, people and peoples have a capacity to choose and create for themselves the terms and conditions on which they will live—and that the role of politicians in shaping the future is therefore fundamental.

During his Prime Ministership, a quotation he once used, that "Life wasn't meant to be easy" was often brought up. While Fraser sometimes joked about the quote, this philosophy—that life confronts humans with challenges that it is up to humans to deal with—was its real meaning. The full quotation deserves a place in this story. Years before he became Prime Minister, in his 1971 Alfred Deakin lecture, Fraser had said:

> Arnold Toynbee once wrote twelve volumes to demonstrate and analyse the cause of the rise and fall of nations. His thesis can be condensed to a sentence, and is simply stated: That through history nations are confronted by a series of challenges and whether they survive or whether they fall to the wayside, depends on the manner and character of their response. Simple, and perhaps one of the few things that is self-evident. It involves a conclusion about the past that life has not been easy for people or for nations, and an assumption for the future that that condition will not alter. There is within me some part of the metaphysic, and thus I would add that life is not meant to be easy.

> I want to add one caution: in writing of the past one ought to be

---

7   Fraser discussed this line of thinking with me on two occasions, both years after he left Parliament. One was in the context of an apparently unpublished article he was writing at the time for a collection of reflections by former world leaders on why they had entered politics. The other was in the context of a discussion about whether it is inevitable that Australia will become a republic.

bound by facts and their interpretation. Similarly, in attempting to draw out the strands of future events one must resist the temptation, which few political philosophers have done, of slipping into a dreamland peopled by races who have few of the characteristics, and none of the failings of the human race.[8]

There is no doubt that this perception of the human situation shaped Fraser's style in government. He did not find it easy to "leave well alone", because history is never really on your side.

His own strength was monumental. Positively, this showed as drive and determination, a capacity to carry matters through to the conclusion he wanted. Negatively, he had a capacity to stand firm and resist pressure. People could find themselves up against a very hard edge. Newspapers often caricatured him with an "Easter Island" image, which raised the unyielding side of Fraser's face almost to iconic status. But he was not inflexible. He constantly sought advice, and he constantly consulted people.

His capacity for work—and consequently his commitment to wide ranging policy involvement—was unflagging. Doug Anthony, the vastly more laid back Deputy Prime Minister, once said of Fraser "If he had a fault, he tried to do too much. He actually worked too hard, he never lets up".[9] Fraser was not in fact a workaholic, for he could easily relax. But as Australia's Prime Minister, he wanted answers to his questions, he wanted action on his decisions, he wanted solutions to the nation's problems! All this added up to a great deal of work, and he was always willing to put in the hours and effort himself. Allied to a remarkable

---

8   See: *Malcolm Fraser on Australia*, pp. 110-11.
9   Ibid, p. 20. Paul Kelly cites part of this comment in his *"John Malcolm Fraser 11 November 1975 - 11 March 1983"* chapter in Grattan, Michelle, (Ed), *Australian Prime Ministers*, New Holland Publishers, Sydney, 2000.

memory, his knowledge was formidable. He once said that he was accustomed to knowing more about a subject than the people he had working on it for him. This set a very high standard all round.

Malcolm Fraser became a stand-out leader. His stature emerged publicly in the context of the 1970s, as he moved beyond the natural reserve which remained a feature of his character. He had what one colleague called natural authority, which led people to get behind him. He had what it takes to be able to attract support. He had what it takes to chart a course for a nation, and to set about going there. He would lead by persuasion, and was not afraid to challenge public opinion. When setting out to shift opinion, he would marshal the facts, determine his line, decide how to express it, then take it to the market place. His persuasive powers were formidable. He would lead from the front, and follow his own convictions. In this sense, he was not a populist leader. He attracted respect rather than affection. He was controversial and he could be abrasive. But the nation knew that it had a leader for a Prime Minister.

He liked to deal in facts. On this basis, he might be described as an 'empiricist'. He was at home with many kinds of facts—economic, political, scientific, moral and emotional. In what he said, he always wanted to provide the relevant facts, especially economic facts. He liked to test propositions against facts. He was lawyer like in his use of evidence—he would sometimes have thousands of pages of evidence searched to find salient information. The foundation even of his legendary opposition to apartheid was essentially factual—that every human being has feelings, and is therefore entitled to consideration. His argument was compelling and persuasive. "How would you feel if you were discriminated against simply because of the colour of your skin", he declaimed to a vast variety of audiences down the years. Without facts, statements are "just words". This factual orientation gave strong discipline and restraint to his thinking.

His mind was analytical. His language was precise, and he was rare among politicians in speaking grammatically flawless sentences off the cuff in parliament. He shaped propositions with precision, and linked them with facts and logic. No academic or abstract thinker, he was powerful and relatively unconfined in argument. He sought from advisers, often in vain, guidelines which derived from wider Liberal values, and which would provide a basis for government policy. Combined with his grasp of affairs, his sense of priorities, and his genuine respect for people and societies, his analytical approach made him an outstanding contributor in discussions at the highest level. His conversations with a person of the calibre of Henry Kissinger, for example, were in a class of their own. Fraser was generally impatient with small talk, though easy in talking about small things that are real. He would unravel loose thinking, and he saw straight through subterfuge, deceit and grandstanding. The chairman of a government authority once started talking to him knowingly about cars, realizing they were a Fraser passion. But Fraser, with two probing questions, and scarcely realizing what he was doing, exposed the line of talk as a total sham.

Fraser was broad in his outlook. No lawyer-politician, his training in the Oxford "PPE" – Philosophy, Politics and Economics —was a potent combination for government. He understood the country and the city, he understood the preoccupations of the different Australian states[10], he understood the priorities of ordinary Australians, he was alive to the concerns and interests of other nations as well as Australia. His interests spanned virtually the whole range of policy.

In understanding Fraser's position in public life, including his relationship with the Liberal Party, it is important to recognize that Fraser was always his own man. In pursuit of his visions, in support of his passions, and in addressing issues he saw as important, he never made life easy, either for himself or others. He liked to follow ideas and arguments where he saw them leading. In this sense, he could never be a pure party loyalist.[11]

All Prime Ministers and political leaders have their own measure of greatness. Fraser's particular views and characteristics were an effective toolkit, not only for handling government, but also for obtaining it.

---

10 After reading my draft for a speech he was to deliver in Perth, Fraser said to me 'You haven't mentioned the Indian Ocean'. Coming from Melbourne, my immediate thought was 'why would the Indian Ocean be mentioned?'. Then I realized that the Indian Ocean, including issues of surveillance, would naturally be an issue worthy of comment in Western Australia in a Prime Ministerial speech – just as the Pacific Ocean is a matter of significance to people who live on Australia's eastern seaboard. This alerted me to Fraser's deep awareness of the diversity of Australia and the differing concerns of people in different parts of our continent.

11 See Patrick Weller's discussion of Fraser's determination in relation to retrospective anti-tax avoidance legislation, which notes Fraser's distaste for tax-avoidance, and states "His was the steel that maintained the commitment (to proceed with anti-avoidance legislation) in the face of violent party opposition. He has still not been forgiven by many in the party for the events of those months." Patrick Weller, *Malcolm Fraser PM: A Study in Prime Ministerial Power in Australia*, Penguin, Ringwood, 1989, p. 393.

Leadership

He came to government in remarkable fashion. After the Labor Party won government in 1972, Billy Snedden became the Liberal Opposition Leader. In the short term, Snedden was successful in rallying the Liberal Party. Two years down the track, it was apparent that he was not up to the job. Parliament often showed its teeth in the 1970s, and it was in Parliament that Labor Prime Minister Whitlam destroyed Snedden. When Whitlam said on 19 February 1975 that Snedden was "without power and without influence", the charge went unanswered.

On 20 March 1975, Malcolm Fraser was elected to replace him as Liberal Leader of the Opposition by a margin of 37 votes to 27. As shown by these figures, the total number of Liberals in the Parliament was not large at the time.

For a capable Opposition Leader, the circumstances were propitious. 1975 was a year of extraordinary tumult in Australian politics, and the Government did not control the Senate. The Australian Political Chronicle illustrates the flavour of the year with its record of the period January to June 1975:

> "Ushered in as it was by cyclone Tracy in Darwin and the collapse of the Tasman bridge in Hobart, this was a half-year of equally stunning political shocks and disasters. Who could have predicted that by the end of June the attorney-general and the minister for defence would have resigned from parliament, that the Speaker of the House of Representatives and the leader of the opposition would be among the backbenchers, and that the treasurer and the minister for labor would be shifted to more junior portfolios? Record unemployment, record inflation, a record government

deficit, the fall of Cambodia and South Vietnam to the communists, and the threat of the Senate again refusing to grant supply created a supercharged atmosphere in which one 'affair' was quickly followed by another.[12]

Fraser turned out to be an unusually successful Leader of the Opposition. The Whitlam Government, less than a year into its second term, was shredded in nine months. There were six steps in Fraser's road to government.

Opposition

First, he cleared the decks. He could easily have been engulfed in speculation about whether he would try to force an early election. As soon as he was elected Opposition Leader, he made an immediate and masterly statement on this issue. His words stood the test of a difficult year, and ultimately spelt disaster for the Whitlam government:

> "The question of supply—let me deal with it this way. I generally believe that if a government is elected to power in the lower House and has the numbers and can maintain the numbers in the lower House, it is entitled to expect that it will govern for the three-year term unless quite extraordinary events intervene. I want to get talk about elections out of the air so the Government can get on with the job of governing and make quite certain that it is not unduly distracted in these particular matters. Having said that, let me also say that if there are questions about when an election might be held or when someone might want to do something about it, I would not be wanting to answer that particular question or trailing my

---
12 In *The Australian Journal of Politics and History*, Vol 21, 1975, pp. 86, 88.

coat about what our tactics or approach might be, because if we do make up our minds at some stage that the Government is so reprehensible that an Opposition must use whatever power is available to it, then I'd want to find a situation in which we made that decision and Mr Whitlam woke up one morning finding the decision had been made..."[13]

It is not surprising that the author of these words had been tutored at Oxford by a Professor of Philosophy who was one of the leading linguistic analysts of his generation.[14] The weight of Fraser's words was exactly balanced. They were reasonable but ominous. They were a gun at the Government's head, but unexceptionable in themselves. Fraser was playing a long political game. There was no malice aforethought, because when he said what he said, the seed that would become the straw that would break the camel's back had not even been sown.[15]

There is no doubt that Malcolm Fraser and Gough Whitlam were the titans of the 1970s. Both almost two metres tall, they were towering figures in the tiny "Old Parliament House". Whitlam was the more flamboyant, Fraser had the sounder judgment. With his pointed words about "extraordinary events" and "reprehensibility", uttered at the very moment of taking up the sword, Fraser actually showed that he already had the measure of the man whose government he would destroy.

Fraser's second step to government was to establish himself as a "Leader with a Direction". He stood out from the first, and it is fair to say that ordinary people immediately sensed what he

---
13 Quoted in Ayres, *Op Cit*, p. 251.
14 Professor Gilbert Ryle, author of *The Concept of Mind*, was one of Fraser's tutors: see Ayres, *op. cit.*, pp. 35 & 70.
15 See below.

was about. He had a lot going for him. He was a striking, youthful figure, fourteen years younger than Whitlam. He was a grazier, with an engaging wife and four young children, and popular interests including classic cars and fishing. There was a great deal on the public record setting out his views, including powerful speeches against the 'big government' tendencies of the 1970s. In a major speech in January 1975, he had highlighted the differences between the socialist and the Liberal—the Labor Party still had a socialist objective at that time—as follows:

> The difference is in attitude of mind... The socialist will turn to government sponsored solutions while the Liberal asks 'can individuals solve it for themselves, can the government create the climate in which that can happen'. Only if the answer is 'no' will the Liberal turn to direct government solutions.[16]

He staked out a view which was unfashionable at the time not only on both sides of Australian politics, but also with conservatives in the UK and the USA:

> The balance between the individual and the state has been overthrown. The state yearly seeks a larger share of resources, people struggle to maintain their share, one group presses against another gaining only momentary advantage while all the time their efforts to preserve themselves against the state actually result in a great addition to the share of the state – at the expense of resources available to individuals. This process results in a withdrawal of effort, a destruction of the work ethic that makes the fabric of the state even more costly to maintain.[17]

---

16 *Malcolm Fraser on Australia*, p.113.
17 Ibid, pp113-14.

Fraser was the first of his generation, both in Australia and internationally, to advocate limited government:

> "Fraser's public commitment to reining in the state pre-dated similar strong campaigns in Britain and the USA by Thatcher and Reagan."[18]

There is one standout number which illustrates the trend that Fraser was opposing. This number is the increase in Commonwealth government expenditure in the 1974-75 Whitlam Government budget. The increase in Commonwealth expenditure in that budget was a staggering nominal 46.4% - 20.4% in real terms.[19] Until Fraser came on the scene, Liberals had opposed the amount of the increase, but not the trend for government spending to spiral upwards. In saying that the trend was wrong and that government needed to be reined in, Fraser clearly and decisively established a new direction.

While the new message of the new Leader of the Opposition was primarily economic, he was surprisingly radical on a number of emerging issues. This made him a vastly more interesting character. For example, because he seemed something of a blue-blood, many people found it hard to come to terms with the fact that he gave priority to environmental protection, and that he had been a foundation member of the Australian Conservation Foundation. He was strongly anti-communist, but he was even more strongly anti-apartheid. It was not easy to stereotype him simply as a conservative who had been born with a silver spoon and sheltered from adversity. In fact, while his childhood was certainly

---

18 Weller, *Op Cit*, p. 273.
19 Reserve Bank of Australia, *Australian Economic Statistics 1949-1950 to 1996-1997, Occasional Paper No. 8*, Table 2.14: Outlays, Receipts and Balance of the Commonwealth Budget.

not deprived, it did include fifteen years of depression, drought and world war. He struck a chord in the minds of the Australian electorate, and he established himself as a clear alternative to the Labor Party.

Fraser's third step to government was to discredit the Whitlam Government. He did this with facts and words taken out of the ministers' own mouths. He used parliament, especially question time, to extract admissions and information which became deadly ammunition in his hands. An exchange on 4 June 1975 with Labor Treasurer Dr Jim Cairns is a classic example. *The Australian Political Chronicle* tells the story:

> In a secret letter to Mr George Harris, dated 7 March 1975 and signed by Dr Cairns, the then treasurer had written that the Australian government would be prepared to pay a brokerage fee of 2 1/2% on a successful negotiation for overseas loan funds. The deputy leader of the opposition (Phillip Lynch) had a copy of that letter when the following exchange took place in the House of Representatives...
>
> Mr LYNCH – I ask the Treasurer – Did he, in a letter dated on or about 5 March, offer a commission of 2 1/2% on any loan money arranged by the recipient of the letter or his company?
>
> Dr J. F. CAIRNS – The answer is no. At no stage did I offer a commission of 2 1/2% or any other amount or give any authority whatever to any person to do anything other than make inquiries.
>
> Mr MALCOLM FRASER – No brokerage fee?
>
> Dr J. F. CAIRNS – No brokerage fee. Would the honourable member like to ask more questions?

> Dr Cairns was shown a copy of the letter on 18 June and Mr Whitlam saw it for the first time on 30 June.[20]

Few people could stand up to a Fraser interrogation. He had an instinct for the information that would be relevant to his cause, and a knack of asking the questions that would draw it out. In this particular case, with the letter in his hand, Fraser was backing a winner with his three deadly words. But his intervention drew the answer which had maximum effect. Cairns was unable to continue as Treasurer. Fraser's questions and probing did similar damage time and again.

Fraser's fourth step to government was to get the existing Government on the run. He was handed a by-election in Tasmania in June, which served the purpose perfectly. The by-election occurred through the resignation, with Whitlam's apparent blessing, of Labor's former deputy leader, Lance Barnard. Fraser's persuasive powers proved formidable, as he blitzed the electorate.

The Bass by-election campaign saw Fraser appealing directly to the people. He always regarded shaping public opinion as a key part of his political job. He had been at it for twenty years in his own electorate of Wannon. Wannon had been a marginal seat before his election, but Fraser made it into one of the jewels in the Liberal crown. He had, for example, taken the trouble to give a five minute radio talk to his electorate every Sunday evening since 1953. Converting the electors of Bass to his cause was therefore not a daunting prospect. He knew that shaping opinion is hard and heavy work, requiring tireless persistence,

---

20 In *The Australian Journal of Politics and History*, Vol 22, 1976, p. 74.

facts, a good "line", and persuasiveness. These were good years for shaping public opinion by argument. He could use the media – television, radio and print—but the medium had not become the message. Fraser was anything but an emotional evangelist - he carried his arguments with facts, substance and strength. In Bass, he put his case in endless speeches to convince the electors.

The Liberal candidate won Bass with a 17.5% swing. This huge result established Fraser's authority in the Liberal Party. It highlighted him as an alternative Prime Minister. It showed how hard it would be for Whitlam to win a third election, especially if that election was held sooner rather than later.

Fraser's fifth step to government was to get a general election at a time when he wanted one. When he became Leader of the Opposition, a General Election was not required for more than two years. In the event, Fraser ultimately determined that there should be a General Election before the Whitlam Government could do more damage or revive its electoral prospects. In Westminster systems, the Prime Minister normally decides when the next election will take place. All the textbooks say that the timing of elections is one of the powers of the Prime Minister. It is a massive power, because the timing impacts the outcome. Australian Prime Ministers have long determined election dates. Even in the case of the 1974 Australian election, when the Liberals had blocked supply, the election timing was substantially decided by Prime Minister Whitlam. In 1975, however, it was Fraser as Leader of the Opposition, rather than Whitlam as Prime Minister, who determined when the next election would take place. This was a crowning achievement, in political terms, for a Leader of the Opposition.

How did Fraser do it? The answer is simple, though the execution was tough. He asked for a general election as a condition of allowing the budget to pass though the Senate. Specifically, he "blocked" supply, i.e. he used his numbers in the Senate to prevent the budget being debated, which meant it could not be voted on.[21] The task Fraser undertook was not just a matter of blocking supply. He had to pick the right moment, and find a cause. He had to use the parliament effectively, particularly the Senate. He had to carry and sustain every last one of his parliamentary colleagues, especially in the Senate. He had to withstand immense pressure, which intensified as soon as he blocked supply, and which tried to force him to back down. He had to handle a hostile media, and soothe the increasingly troubled organizational wing of the Liberal Party. He had to judge correctly how the Governor-General—a Whitlam appointee—would handle the situation. He had to judge correctly the resources which an imperious Prime Minister with his back to the wall would be able to marshal.

The rightness or wrongness of what Fraser did will long be debated. There has always been a close correlation between people's views on this question, and their political persuasion. It is important to separate Fraser's role from that of the Governor-General. While there were strongly voiced views when Fraser blocked supply that he should not have done so, there had equally been strongly voiced views beforehand that Whitlam should have called an election when he could not get supply. Whatever the complex of motives and reasons in Fraser's own mind, there

---

[21] The story of the blocking of supply and the constitutional crisis is told in many places, e.g. Ayres, *Op. Cit.*, pp 271-301, tells it very much from the Fraser viewpoint. The present account deals with it in the context of Fraser securing a general election.

is no doubt that he was urgently and legitimately concerned about Australia's future. The fact that it took so many years to get Australia out of its economic mess remains clear evidence for that. Fraser's actions amounted, in their practical effect, to a political *tour de force* of monumental proportions.

Fraser needed to find the right moment to block supply, and there needed to be a straw to break the camel's back—something new that was extraordinary and reprehensible. These requirements came together at the time when the Government brought the Budget into the Senate in early October 1975, where there would have been a debate over several days. But on 13 October, there was a newspaper revelation that the Minister for Minerals and Energy had continued to pursue a loan of several billion dollars after his authority to do so had been withdrawn.[22] It was a dramatic story, with telexes, statutory declarations, and the appearance that Parliament had been misled. The Minister for Minerals and Energy was forced to resign on 14 October.

With this revelation, it would in effect have been a backdown for Fraser not to pull the trigger. Who knows what would have happened if the Minister had stayed within his authority? Fraser's shadow ministry and parliamentary colleagues backed him in the idea of pulling the trigger by blocking supply. Step by step, the pieces came into place. That having been done, he held his colleagues and the rest of the party together. He resisted the pressure to back down, which was immense. He made no mistake about Whitlam's resources, or the Governor-General's approach if and when the decision came to him.

---

22 For a fuller discussion of the "Loans Affair", see Ayres, *Op. Cit.*, pp 261-65, 273-74, and passim.

Following four weeks of maneuvering, the Governor General dismissed Gough Whitlam as Prime Minister on 11 November 1975, and a general election was called. Thus Malcolm Fraser surmounted his fifth step to government—getting a general election at a time when he wanted it. In effect, Fraser had confronted a challenge proactively, he had analysed the issues soundly, he had dealt with the facts—these, and indeed all his other key qualities and characteristics, had been brought into play in this huge political act.

The sixth and final step to government was to win the election. After the preceding tumult, and despite bitterness, this in effect became a formality. The real issue was whether people would vote on the economy or the constitutional crisis. Fraser campaigned on the economy, and his judgment in doing so was again vindicated. Overwhelmingly, the electors voted on the economy. The coalition parties won 57% of the two-party preferred vote. They won 91 seats out of 127 in the House of Representatives. They won 35 seats out of 64 in the Senate.[23]

Malcolm Fraser thus became Prime Minister on 13 December 1975, with control of both houses, and record majorities. But this did not give him unlimited power. The road ahead would turn out to be harder than he or others had anticipated. It will be appropriate, in considering the Fraser Governments, to be selective, because many consuming issues of those days have lost their interest. The opening paragraph of this work identified the achievements and concerns which have enduring interest. They require varied treatment, and they deserve different

---

23 *The Australian Political Chronicle*, *The Australian Journal of Politics and History*, Vol 22, 1976, p. 81.

emphases. This account starts with the situation in which Fraser found himself. It then explores the whole issue of restraining government. This is followed with an overview of other domestic initiatives which are worthy of remembrance. Fourth, the significance of some key activities in the international arena is highlighted.

Government

What was Fraser's situation, and how powerful was the Government's position? In Australia, strong majorities in both Houses of Federal Parliament do not give unlimited power to the Government. In Fraser's case, Australia was still digesting the massive changes of the Whitlam era. New democratic governments cannot simply reverse the actions of their predecessors and turn the way they want. In addition, Fraser had to deal with the division and bitterness which arose from the way he had won government and Labor had lost it. This required careful management. In Australia, the power and authority of Federal Governments is limited not only by the Constitution and the States, but also by strong institutions including Trades Unions, Employer Organizations, and pressure groups. The Media, the Opposition, the Backbench, the Party Organizations, Public Opinion – all impose constraints on the Government, no matter how large its parliamentary majority.

What any Government achieves needs to be understood in the context of its position, and what Machiavelli called "the spirit of the times". One common criticism of Fraser, particularly from business, was always that he did not "take on the unions". It is an issue worth dwelling on. The Commonwealth's powers over unions are limited by the Constitution, and it was by no means clear that "taking the unions on" was the best way to tame them. Fraser certainly started with a more conciliatory approach. Overall, while Fraser may have been able to do more or better than he did, he certainly made extensive use of the powers that were available to him: the Government established an Industrial Relations Bureau; it introduced secret ballots in union elections and for strike action; it established a National Labor Consultative Council; it legislated to increase the Commonwealth's power over its own employees; it banned secondary boycotts. It should not be overlooked that for most of Fraser's Prime Ministership, the Trade Union movement was led by Bob Hawke, a popular and powerful figure who was never going to lie down in the face of Coalition majorities in Parliament.

Fraser's own dissatisfaction with what was achieved in this arena was obvious from the fact that he made an election promise in the 1983 campaign to hold a referendum to give the Commonwealth constitutional power over industrial relations. He must surely have realized that he had no hope of getting nationwide approval for such a major increase in Commonwealth power. The fact that he proposed it not only reflected his own frustration. It demonstrated that large majorities in both Houses of Parliament had not given him the power to deal with unions as he would or might have wished.

In the larger perspective, the limitations in practice of parliamentary power were also evident from reactions to certain Fraser Government cost-cutting measures. It was not just the Labor Party that was critical. When the media strikes a chord which is in tune with community opinion in criticizing a government initiative, there is often little alternative but for the Government to back down. This was the fate of a number of Fraser Government proposals, including as an example, an ill-fated and probably ill-conceived measure to remove payment of funeral benefits.

There was a catch in the position in which Fraser found himself, as the spirit of the times evolved throughout his period of office. The catch was this:

- on the one hand, Fraser came to office on a platform of Government doing less, i.e. needing to be reduced;
- at the same time, Fraser recognised that Government is limited in what it can do;
- the catch, which he did not sufficiently recognize, was that Government is constrained even in what it can do to reduce its own operations.

This constraint was partly due to the difficulty of unraveling the big expectations created by big government. It was also partly due to the resistance which came from the beneficiaries of government programs which were being cut or eliminated. Had Fraser realized how hard it would be to reduce the size of government, he might have been more restrained in promising reductions.

The problem was compounded by the fact that Fraser tried to persuade the community to expect less from government, and in particular to expect less government spending. This message was widely well received, particularly by business. But the more he persuaded business to expect that government would do less and that it should spend less, the more business was unhappy with him when it was found the job was harder than he or anyone else had realized.

Overall, therefore, despite his large majorities, Fraser's power was subject to a number of restraints. At the same time, against the background of the excess and adventurism of the Whitlam economic measures, the economic challenge facing Australia was profound. It was presumably for this reason that Sir Robert Menzies had described the 1975 election as "The most vital Australian election in my time"[24]. The effects of the 20.4% 'real' (46.4% 'nominal') increase in Government spending in the 1974-75 budget were still running through the economy.[25] While the 1975-76 Labor budget had been widely hailed as restrained, it nevertheless increased Commonwealth spending substantially. Furthermore, the projected 1975-76 deficit of $2.8b had increased to $4b by the time of the 1975 election. These numbers seemed – and were—huge at that time.

Restraint, responsibility and reduction of government were key themes that Fraser emphasised both when he obtained office, and throughout his Prime Ministership. These are enduring themes from a liberal perspective, because in a fundamental sense, less government means more freedom. Fraser's role in persuading Australians to expect responsibility and restraint from Government on the one hand, and on the other hand not to expect too much from Government, were decisive achievements at a crucial time. They occasioned a seachange in Australian federal politics.

---
24 Ayres, *Op. Cit.*, p. 301.
25 Reserve Bank of Australia, *Australian Economic Statistics 1949-1950 to 1996-1997, Occasional Paper No. 8*, Table 2.14: Outlays, Receipts and Balance of the Commonwealth Budget.

These achievements brought about a fundamental undermining of a socialist approach, which forced the federal Labor Party to move closer to the Liberal Party and thus shifted the centre of gravity of Australian politics. To the extent that this impacted the Hawke and Keating Governments, their impact on Australia was substantially different from earlier Labor approaches. To illustrate this, had these Commonwealth Labor Governments followed the pattern of the Victorian Labor Governments in the 1980s and early 1990s[26], rather than the more restrained Fraser approach, Australia would have gone in a very different direction.

This is not the whole of the ledger. It is important to look more broadly at the character of Fraser's commitments to reduction, responsibility and restraint, including the outcomes that eventuated, and the way in which the theme was itself transformed throughout his period of office. It is a complex story.

Throughout his Prime Ministership, Fraser saw economic management as his foremost responsibility. Good economic management required restraint. This was partly but not wholly because of excessive government spending before he came to office. His commitment was to the reduction or containment of government expenditure, of taxation, and of the deficit. These objectives linked with getting the fundamentals of the economy right, particularly inflation and employment. His commitment to expenditure restraint and government reduction could never of course be isolated from his convictions about the positive role which government needed to play. But it was, overall, a decisive and enduring commitment.

---

26 To illustrate, in 1990, the Victorian State Government only saved the State Bank of Victoria from collapse by selling it to the Commonwealth Bank.

Taxing and Spending

Fraser talked up his commitment to expenditure restraint strongly and convincingly throughout his period of office. Perhaps its most profound and potentially far-reaching component was his initial commitment to tax indexation. Particularly in an inflationary environment and with a stepped tax system, this is the true basis of government restraint. Tax indexation would probably do more than anything else to maintain a desirable liberal balance between the demands of the state on the one hand, and the claims of the individual and private enterprise on the other. Tax indexation would be as "real" to government - if it could be entrenched — as "taxes and death" are "real" to citizens. Fraser made serious initial attempts to give reality to his rhetoric. But more or less full indexation was quickly reduced to half indexation, and then it was dropped altogether. What did remain –— and it has not been altered since — was bringing the top tax rate below 50%. In retrospect, tax indexation was a bold initiative, which would have imposed a permanent hobble on Government revenue, and which was probably therefore ultimately utopian. Subsequent governments have not reverted to it. Tax indexation never seems to have had the electoral popularity it surely deserved from a liberal perspective.

In simple terms, the core of government restraint in Australia relates to Commonwealth expenditure. Fraser remained committed to holding government expenditure down throughout his period of office. It was not a popular long-term commitment, because it always seemed negative and nobody seemed to benefit directly. It fell to Fraser, even more than to the Treasurer or Finance Minister, to make a continuing stand for expenditure restraint. Fraser went to great lengths to keep his finger on the pulse of expenditure.[27] Patrick Weller notes in relation to the first Fraser Government budget, which held real growth in expenditure to 0.8%[28], that:

> "No contemporary observer commented that the budget represented a lost opportunity, that the government could have – or should have — cut harder".[29]

Few of Fraser's critics remembered that nobody thought he could have cut harder than he did in that first budget!

Fraser continued to emphasise the importance of expenditure restraint throughout his Prime Ministership — even in his final budget, which loosened the reins with 7.1% real growth in Commonwealth expenditure.[30] This budget was handed down in the context of recession, drought, and an upcoming election — so a more forgiving approach is hardly surprising. Compared with Fraser's 7.1%, the highest real increase for a single year in the McMahon period was 5.1%; for Whitlam it was 20.4%; for Hawke 8.5%; for Keating 5.4%.[31] Fraser's relative largesse in his Government's final budget certainly did not make ordinary electors think him generous.

By the wholly quantitative measure of "real growth in outlays in the Commonwealth Budget", the average annual rate of increase during the Fraser years – difficult as these years were – was 2.2%

---

27 Weller, *Op Cit.*, pp. 214ff.
28 Reserve Bank of Australia, *Loc Cit.*
29 Weller, *Op Cit.*, p 230.
30 Reserve Bank of Australia, *Loc Cit.*
31 Reserve Bank of Australia, *Loc Cit.*

for the seven Fraser budgets.[32] This compares with 4.8% for the McMahon period (two budgets), 10.5% for the Whitlam period (three budgets), 2.3% for the Hawke period (nine budgets), and 3.7% for the Keating period (four budgets).

The influence of the Fraser government on the Hawke government in the matter of government expenditure growth is a matter for conjecture. But there would be little argument that Hawke had to measure himself against the Fraser performance rather than the Whitlam performance.

A telling qualitative measure of the size of government is "Commonwealth Budget outlays as a proportion of GDP". This measure states how much of the total national cake the Commonwealth government takes. Over his seven years, Fraser held the size of government against this testing measure.[33] This proportion had risen under Whitlam by a hefty 5.9 percentage points, from 22.7% in the last McMahon budget to 28.6 % in the last Whitlam budget. Fraser got it down to 25.8% in his fourth and fifth budgets. This was a useful gain, for it is far harder to lower than to lift this figure. The subsequent combination of slow growth and higher expenditure eroded the gain, first to 26.2% in Fraser's sixth budget, then back to the starting point of 28.6% in his last.

The ongoing prominence which Fraser gave to expenditure restraint can be perceived from an initiative which followed the 1980 election. This was the notorious "Review of Commonwealth Functions", whose purpose was "to identify functions which

---

32 Reserve Bank of Australia, *Loc Cit*. This and the subsequent figures have been reached by taking an arithmetical average of the each year's % real growth in budget outlays.
33 The figures which follow are from Reserve Bank of Australia, *Loc Cit*.

were not necessary or which could be more appropriately performed by the private sector".[34] Some people still remember this review, forty years later. It was popularly—or unpopularly—known as "The Razor Gang". It was never likely to be a popular initiative, and the fact that Fraser persisted with it testifies to his commitment to government restraint. The Review was in the end something of a damp squib, although the idea of Government "selling off" functions and organizations subsequently gathered considerable momentum.

Deregulation

Deregulation was a further dimension of government restraint and reduction. Fraser generally supported the idea of reducing the burden of government regulation. But he also believed that Government needed to secure a framework which would allow private enterprise to flourish, and at the same time be consistent with the preservation of the social fabric—including a fair go for everyone, while taking account of the needs of the country as well as the city, of smaller states as well as larger states. Financial deregulation was an emerging issue during the Fraser period which came to assume critical importance. It was linked with a debate within the Liberal Party itself about the need to foster a more open economy.

Fraser set Australia on the road to financial deregulation through the establishment of the influential Campbell Committee inquiry. But he did not take Australia on the journey. When the Campbell report came in, the Fraser Government

---

34 Patrick Weller, *Op cit*, p 245.

was actually only 16 months away from the 1983 election. Implementation of the Campbell Report was going to be both controversial and complex. In the end, it was left to the next government to make the journey which was recommended.[35] It is not clear how far the Fraser Government would have wanted to go, even if time had not been allowed to slip away.

The Campbell report broke a lot of ground which is commonplace now, but new then. It contained an integrated set of recommendations, and neither Fraser nor several of his ministers agreed with all of them. A more competitive and market oriented financial system was the objective, and it might be expected that a Liberal Government would have given relatively unreserved support to this. On the other hand, the report treated a number of entrenched social objectives – such as government support for home ownership – as extraneous factors which should be set on one side. The approach actually signaled a tremendous shift in political priorities, which was to develop into the globalism whose dynamic became so widely taken for granted early in the Twenty First Century. The issue of how to protect the weak, and how to restrain the strong, would have remained issues of enduring concern for Fraser had he continued in office, and he continued to tackle them from the sidelines for the rest of his life.

Overall, because Fraser made ground on the most testing measure of government restraint, because he highlighted the importance of fiscal responsibility so firmly, and because he turned opinion around so decisively in persuading people to

---

35 The Hawke government actually needed a further report – the Martin report – before it undertook its journey.

expect less of government, Fraser's commitment to government restraint stands as an outstanding feature of his Prime Ministership.

A significant number of other enduring initiatives and innovations in Australian life came out of the Fraser years, and therefore bear his stamp. Six of these are singled out for comment.

Human Dignity, the Constitution and the Environment

Fraser instituted Aboriginal Land Rights legislation, building on earlier moves. This legislation gave inalienable freehold title to Aboriginal people living in traditional tribal areas. The Government also promoted a self-management approach, as opposed to the more paternalistic approach of earlier times.[36] The land rights legislation resulted in Aboriginal ownership of very substantial areas of Australia. It was thus an important step in the process, which he described in 1978 as unavoidably requiring "long term effort", "because of generations of neglect and discrimination against Aboriginals in education, health, employment and housing", to "achieve nothing less than real equality of all Australians – equality of rights, equality of opportunities, equality of protection under the law".[37] These were matters about which he felt profoundly and deeply.

Fraser played a key role in the institutionalisation and acceptance of Australia as a multicultural society. Multiculturalism, now taken for granted as one of Australia's

---
36 See Ayres, *Op Cit.*, p. 371-2.
37 *Malcolm Fraser on Australia*, p. 104.

greatest strengths, was novel and quite widely perceived as a threat to Australian values at the time when Fraser was in government. Multiculturalism replaced the policy of assimilation.

Fraser constantly hammered the theme that "loyalty to and love of Australia were in no way incompatible with deep affection for one's homeland".[38] Fraser had spoken on this theme as far back as 1969. In government, he put his weight strongly behind multiculturalism, including the commissioning of the Galbally inquiry and acceptance of its 57 recommendations, and the establishment of multicultural television (SBS). While the credit for multiculturalism must be shared, nobody was more instrumental than Fraser both in its establishment and making it a part of mainstream Australia.

Fraser introduced family allowances in the first budget. This was a simple example of lateral thinking, based on a search for fairness, and partly motivated by a desire to sugar some bitter pills in an austere situation. There had previously been a system of child endowment, which operated as a tax deduction. Because tax rates were progressive, the old system of child endowment was worth most to high income earners, and it was worth nothing to non-income earners. The cost to the Government of introducing family allowances, which were paid to everyone, was virtually balanced out by the abolition of child endowment.[39] The benefit to needy families was absolute, because family allowances targetted families with less income.

On the constitutional front, the Fraser Government

---

38 See Ayres, *Op Cit.*, p. 138.
39 Reserve Bank of Australia, *Loc Cit*, footnote (g)

sponsored three successful referendums for constitutional reform, more than any other Government since Federation. The first change required state governments to fill casual Senate vacancies with appointees from the same party. The second imposed a retiring age of 70 on judges. The third gave electors living in Territories a vote in referendums. They were all practical referendums with a democratic thrust. Without the Senate vacancies reform, the Constitution would have been seriously disfigured. Fraser's approach to constitutional change was incremental rather than reformist. His strong sense of what would—and would not – convince ordinary people rarely deserted him. He was very conscious that a referendum which increased Canberra's power had little chance of success. Fraser also conducted a plebiscite to choose a new national anthem, and in this sense "Advance Australia Fair" was democratically chosen – the other options were "God Save the Queen" and "Waltzing Matilda".

The decision to build Parliament House was a Fraser Government initiative, and Fraser allowed it to continue even when cutting costs in other areas. It is an interesting case, because putting money into buildings which will benefit politicians is not likely to endear a government to the Australian electorate. Fraser himself always thought that the design was the key. The imagination of the nation was captured by the fact that the building was underground—under lawns which citizens could walk across—which meant that ordinary Australians could walk all over their politicians. It is fitting that this great building is nobody's monument.

The Fraser Government made a number of landmark

environmental decisions, at a time when a Liberal government might have been expected to be more equivocal. The list is substantial: protection of the Great Barrier Reef, strong support for Australia's first World Heritage listings, development of national parks including the proclamation of Kakadu National Park, the ban on whaling, the elimination of mining on Fraser Island, are major examples. It was not a one way street, and in some situations—as in the Tasmanian Government plan to allow part of the Tasmanian wilderness to be destroyed to build a power station—Fraser was not willing to override the State government. The sincerity and seriousness of Fraser's commitment helped to entrench environmental protection in the Australian consciousness.

International

Fraser's energies and interests in the international arena were wide-ranging, spanning security, trade, racism, refugees, and Australia's regional position. His role in welcoming refugees—particularly many who had bravely fled Vietnam in tiny boats—was characteristic of his breadth and compassion. This particular initiative won him prodigious appreciation, and cemented his lifelong resolve to push the case for refugees.

With the end of the cold war and the abolition of apartheid, some major preoccupations of the Fraser years have passed into history, although the big international issues take different shapes in different eras. It is illuminating to look closely at Fraser's methodology in the international arena, at his view of Australia's role and position, and how he was viewed in this context by some illustrious peers.

Henry Kissinger wrote that Fraser was "not a practitioner of classical power politics, though he understands the importance of power. In his attitude toward equal justice in Southern Africa, he has consistently made clear that in a democracy foreign policy must reflect the moral convictions of its people".[40] Fraser certainly saw himself as having a fundamental concern for people, and thus he did not think of international affairs as like moving pieces on a board. Kissinger also highlighted Fraser's realism, understanding, and farsighted approach to developments in the Pacific and Asia, noting that the axis of world politics would shift to the Pacific in something more than a generation, and that Australia will then be "at the vortex of world affairs".

Fraser was sensitive to nuance in international affairs. He knew the value of adapting to the tone of major leaders in order to create a meeting of minds. He took every opportunity to meet other heads of government. In 1981, when walking out of Claridge's hotel in London after the wedding of Prince Charles and Princess Diana, Fraser noticed another party entering the hotel. He said he thought the leader of this party was President Sadat of Egypt—and so it was. An impromptu meeting, which lasted for an hour, was immediately arranged at Fraser's request. This accident of history certainly influenced Fraser's views about Australian participation in a peacekeeping force in the Sinai.

While conscious of Australia's limited position, Fraser was

---

40 *Malcolm Fraser on Australia*, p. xvi.

prepared to set Australia's sights high in international affairs. In 1982, he proposed an ambitious four-pronged proposal to overcome world recession.[41] This proposal was addressed to the major western nations meeting at a Versailles economic summit. He publicised the proposal during a visit to the United States, where, as in other forums, he emphasised Australia's positive international contribution, both in wars and in peacekeeping.

Fraser was willing to hammer constantly at major themes. He attacked apartheid endlessly, never referring to Africa without developing a full-blown argument against apartheid. This particular persistence paid off profoundly. It helped to influence the eventual outcome in South Africa. More immediately, it enhanced Australia's standing and perceived independence in the minds of many Asian countries, where the old White Australia policy was still a sensitive issue.

Fraser conceptualised Australia as a "middle ranking power". A middle ranking power has "influence". It lacks the power to impose its will in most matters, but it can nevertheless count for something. Moreover, if it proceeds cleverly, a "middle ranking" power can leverage its influence. The 1981 issue of the Sinai Peacekeeping Force was a classic example. The United States was trying to put together a multi-nation peacekeeping force to support a Middle Eastern peace process, but no other significant countries were holding up their hands to join the force. Fraser saw the peace process as in Australia's interest. He therefore wanted to ensure that a multi-nation peacekeeping force was established, and he was willing for Australia to take part. But he was not prepared to go it alone with the Americans.

---

41 The proposal is amplified in *Ibid*, pp. 85-86.

The decision which the Fraser government took, which was communicated in advance to the Americans, was to commit Australia to participating in the peacekeeping force, but only on the condition that two other substantial powers also joined the force. Australia alone would not have been able to persuade other major countries to join. But the United States was able to use Australia's conditional commitment as a lever to persuade two other major countries to join its proposed force. As a result, through leveraging its influence, Australia was able to secure the outcome it wanted, and also help a great ally to secure a result which it was finding difficult on its own.

This approach highlighted the seriousness of Australia's international commitments. Leading international visitors were impressed at the self-confidence which they perceived in Australia at the opening of the 1980s.

The 1982 world recession for which Fraser had sought an international circuit breaker persisted despite his best efforts. Its impact on Australia was compounded by a drought. As 1982 moved forward, the election that was not due until late in 1983 loomed increasingly large, and options began to close in. Although Labor Leader Bill Hayden said that "a drover's dog" could win the next election for Labor, there were doubts about whether Hayden could beat Fraser. At the same time, Bob Hawke was vying for the Labor leadership. Fraser probably knew that he could not overcome Hawke's popularity, particularly if the run up to the election was short.

Moving On

Certainly in retrospect, the Fraser Government's time was running out. With an ironic twist, Fraser's decision to seek an early election coincided with the day of the election of Hawke to the leadership of the Labor Party. A serious drought persisted – and then the Ash Wednesday bushfires supervened during the campaign. It was no surprise that Labor had a clear win in the election.

Fraser immediately made the decision that he would not seek re-election as Liberal leader. Contenders for that position had long been waiting in the wings. Partly because he felt his presence might be seen as divisive, Fraser decided soon afterwards to resign from the Parliament.

This change ushered in the next phase of his life, where for more than thirty years he was a prolific commentator, speaker and writer on policy and world events. This included publishing a substantial volume of *Memoirs* and two further books,[42] while also playing various significant public roles including leading an "Eminent Persons" group to South Africa to seek the abolition of apartheid. To the end, Fraser remained a force in Australian affairs – always able to command a newspaper headline when he felt an issue mattered, always ready to stand up for what he felt was right, always "for Australia" – and "a fair go"!

---

[42] Details of Fraser's three books are cited in the bibliography.

Malcolm Fraser Quotations[43]

Priorities

"The individual happiness of each citizen is, and must remain for ever, the first thought of our national leaders."

(Maiden Speech, 22 Feb 1956)

"Scientific knowledge has placed unparalleled power in politicians' hands. Our capacity to see that it is used for good is scarcely better than it would have been if mankind had possessed that power two thousand years ago."

(Endowing a Chair in Australian Studies at Harvard Univ, 30 July 1976, p 131)

"There is obviously a great deal that can be said on the subject of equality of employment opportunity in our community, but one matter on which there is surely no doubt is that every future history of our times will give a significant place to the subject of women in the workforce... The full significance of the changes that have been taking place is not easy to assess, and while it is not easy to find an historical benchmark from which to start, I find some interest in the fact that in the original Liberal Party platform of 1946 there is a section entitled 'Status of Women' which contains the following simple

---

[43] Page references are to *Malcolm Fraser on Australia*.

but comprehensive statement: *'Equality of opportunities, liberties and status for men and women'*. These words were farsighted in several ways..."

(Businesswoman of the Year Award, Sydney, 16 November 1981, p 117)

"Throughout all our work together we must never forget that any policy based on the superiority of one race over another is a policy doomed to failure."

(The National Aboriginal Conference, Canberra, 3 April 1978, p 104)

"(Multiculturalism) sees diversity as a quality to be actively embraced, a source of social wealth and dynamism. It encourages groups to be open and to interact, so that all Australians may learn and benefit from each other's heritages."

(Inauguration of the Institute of Multicultural Affairs, Melbourne, 30 November 1981, p 106)

"The concept of economic interdependence is not without its ambiguities... (But) our fates are inextricably intertwined, and in the contemporary world no society is an economic island. A full recognition of the... urgent need for a greater accommodation of developing countries within the global economy is vital, both in political and economic terms."

(CHOGM, Lusaka, 2 August 1979, p 69)

"We don't want big government, nor do the Australian people... Limited government has a far greater capacity to improve care for those who need assistance... Society has immense resources for achieving what people want without the need for counterproductive intrusion by governments."

(Australian Liberal Students Federation, 15 May 1981, pp 111-12)

"The great task of statesmanship is to apply past lessons to new situations, to draw correct analogies to understand and act upon present forces, to recognise the need for change. We must be particularly aware of the great weakness of human idealism which is to forget the frailty of the human race..."

(Alfred Deakin Lecture at The University of Melbourne, 20 July, 1971, p. 102)

"Man is part of the natural environment, and while man surely has the right to utilise the resources of this planet, a critical question is how best to use these resources to enhance the quality of human life, and avoid unacceptable damage to our physical and cultural heritage. It is certainly not acceptable for this generation to rob the next, or for us to pass on to our children a less healthy, a less beautiful, or a less enriching heritage than we enjoy ourselves."

(World Heritage Committee Meeting, 26 October 1981, p 215)

"It is widely accepted that the interests of Australia are not advanced by disagreement between the major parties on fundamental questions affecting our nation's security."

(Electorate Talk, 12 April 1982, p 24)

Australia

"Our greatest strength of all, the one which underpins all the rest, is the capacity of Australians to keep building Australia up, and the capacity of governments such as ours to provide the conditions in which they can do so."

(Liberal Party Lunch in Sydney, 23 April 1982, p 104)

"Our own efforts are going to be the main determinants of the kind of Australia we create"

(Hobart Press Club, 27 October 1976, p 103)

"All institutions and all organizations, especially the large ones, should be fully subject to the rule of law, and fully amenable to rules that prevent these institutions and organisations from trampling on the rights and the liberties of other Australians."

(Liberal Party Dinner in Melbourne, 7 June 1983, p 126)

Economic Matters

"Under conditions of market freedom, individuals have more power than under any other form of economic organisation. In a market economy individuals can choose where they will work, and for whom; what they will buy, and when... In exercising their freedom to choose, they create over time an economy and a society which is more likely to adjust to their needs than one which is centrally controlled."

(Melbourne Chamber of Commerce, 26 March 1981, p. 124)

"Australians' commitment to free enterprise is not founded simply on the fact that it is the most economic system available, or the most efficient provider of the resources required to produce a better life for all Australians... There is a consensus of support for free enterprise because it is the most democratic system. It confers on the individual maximum freedom of choice; it allows the individual maximum opportunity to innovate, to strike out on his own, to try out his own schemes and dreams; it makes the individual consumer the ultimate arbiter of taste, the ultimate allocator of resources."

(Opening of Enterprise Week in Melbourne, 24 October 1977, p 122)

"... Much government regulation of private sector activity is neither necessary nor effective and is certainly more costly than is self-regulation."

(On the release of 'Razor Gang' Report, 30 April 1981, p 200)

The World

"Whatever view one takes of China's ideology, it is clear that Chinese society manifests a sense of purpose and self-reliance. A stable equilibrium in international relations is not possible unless China is more fully involved in the international community."

(National Press Club, Washington, 29 July 1976, p. 54)

"So much depends on the President of the United States that if he embarks on a course which we believe advances our ideals we should say so. He depends on the support of a Congress which is in turn greatly influenced by American opinion. The American people in turn are influenced by their awareness of what people in other countries are thinking."

(Zionist Council of Victoria, Melbourne, 3 May 1981, p 48)

"All varieties of terrorists are to be condemned. Terrorism constitutes a systematic assault on the most fundamental of human rights; the right to live in a physically secure environment and the right to hold contrary views... The terrorist is an extremist obsessed by his own ideas, ready to use any means; impervious to moral scrutiny, criticism or restraint."

(Inaugural Sir Robert Menzies Lecture, Monash University, 30 March 1978, p. 67-8)

Democracy

"The private Member of Parliament – the member who sits on the backbench – is a key and central figure in the parliamentary democracy we enjoy in Australia. The private member... is a barometer of public attitudes because of his intimate links with his constituents. He is able to quickly sense a community need and bring that to the attention of government. No government can afford not to heed his advice and his concerns."

(Electorate Talk, 20 May 1979, pp 133-34)

'If the people cannot call to account the makers of government policy, they ultimately have no way of controlling public policy, or the impact of that policy on their own lives."

(Garran Memorial Oration, 14 November 1977, p 135)

"Despite the possibility of failure, a willingness to look reality in the face shows that the diversity of opinion and the wide distribution of power that are characteristic of democracies are not merely compatible with an effective foreign policy, but in the proper combinations, they are resources of unparalleled potency."

(Roy Milne Memorial Lecture, Sydney, 27 September 1976, p 34)

The Media

"Newspapers are not meant to make politicians happy."

(Canberra Times 50th anniversary, 22 September 1976, p. 168)

"Without press freedom, the standards set by any government will decline, the worth and quality of government policies will deteriorate. With this freedom comes responsibility. A responsibility to expose; to criticise; to distinguish fact from opinion; to be honest and fairminded in the presentation of opinion. But the responsibility is greater than this. There is now a responsibility to examine the effects of the press on the fibre of the nation, whether it fosters dispute or division, whether it enhances community spirit and pride. It is the ability to fuse criticism with this equally important sense of responsibility that is the hallmark of a free press at its best."

(International Press Institute, Canberra, March 1978)

Learning and Education

"I believe that books will never be surpassed or replaced as the essential foundation for serious study."

(Opening of the International Booksellers Federation Congress, 23 March 1981, p 170)

"Our enjoyment of freedom will depend greatly on the quality of our educational system and the values our educators impart... Education, and the appropriate pattern of the educational system will, whatever our views, be one of the major issues facing the Australian people for the foreseeable future."

(Liberal Party Federal Council, Canberra, 19 September 1976, p. 221)

"What we need now, more than ever, is knowledge which is of positive value to man in increasing his understanding of the world. Our education needs to impart not only technical skills, it needs to impart a quality of judgement."

(Endowment of a Chair at Harvard, 30 July 1976, p 221)

"Australia has enormous technological potential... We should be concerned with the recognition given to technologists... Too often, technologists have been seen as following a lesser occupation, a lesser profession than that of research scientists. But the effort, the ability, the creative skills required in technological innovation are of the same order as those of the scientist... Australia has an enormous store of technological knowledge and expertise in academic institutions, government and industry. Our aim now must be to transfer this information to Australian enterprises which can use it to increase their efficiency and develop new products.'

(Australian Academy of Technological Sciences, Canberra, 31 October 1978, p. 219)

"Unfortunately, it is a fact that in recent times, academic freedom has been threatened. It is sometimes easier to make a speech on the Melbourne waterfront, before members of the Waterside Workers Federation, than it is to get a hearing on some tertiary campuses. The plain fact is that members of a union with one of Australia's most radical traditions are more ready to listen to argument and debate, than a minority of students who believe that they have the right to suppress views different from their own. If the views of this tiny minority of students prevail, then the academic freedom of tertiary institutions will have been undermined by their own members, and much of the sympathy which the wider community has for universities and colleges will be forfeited."

(Melbourne State College, 21 February 1977, p 227)

Freedom

"In formulating policy, one thing which we recognise very clearly, and it distinguishes us decisively, is the vitality of freedom in advancing people's dignity and self-respect... Freedom permits change, and thus prevents the build-up of the kinds of frustrations and tensions... which are never far from the surface in any socialist country."

(Policy Assembly of the Victorian Liberal Party, 7 August 1981, p 119)

"I want to say to young people in particular, make no assumptions which suggest that the future lies outside human control. Such assumptions would be unworthy of your own capacities – and of the responsibilities which you owe to the generations which will follow you."

(Australian Liberal Students Federation, 15 May 1981, p 112)

Equality

"We must achieve nothing less than real equality of all Australians – equality of rights, equality of opportunities, equality of protection under the law."

(The National Aboriginal Conference, Canberra, 3 April 1978, p 104)

Security

"There are risks, especially in a democracy, in coming to decisions which have to be based on assessments which cannot be proved, but in an uncertain world, taking such risks is sometimes well justified. Henry Kissinger... recently made a comment which is very relevant to this. 'Often', he said, 'expertise consists of management of the familiar while society needs a vision of a future that no one has yet experienced'."

NSW State Zionist Council, 22 April 1982, p 64)

"In the kind of world we are living in, it is all the more important for nations of goodwill, which have learnt the art of compromise through their own democratic processes, which are committed to consensus and reconciliation rather than confrontation, to carry those principles into international affairs."

(Hansard, in a statement on the international situation, 22 February 1979, pp 40-41)

Responsibility

"Children need to know, and want to know, what is permissible and what is not. Families who believe they can raise children in an environment devoid of rules risk the moral development of their children and their capacity to adjust successfully to the demands of an adult world. There is no doubt that a family model will always be the basis for a child's learning."

(School Opening in Sydney, 4 May 1980, p. 221)

The value of sport

"One of the greatest things about sportsmen and women is that they are achievers."

(25th Anniversary of the Melbourne Olympics, 22 Nov 1981, p 233)

Rights

"...While the law has a vital role to play in the protection of rights, human rights in the end are a matter of attitudes and relationships between people."

(Inauguration of the Human Rights Commission, Canberra, 10 December 1981, p 228)

Art

"Art, like justice, should not only be done, but should also be seen to be done. It must be available to the people."

(Opening the Genesis of a Gallery exhibition in Canberra, 9 March 1977, p 233)

Australia's International Voice

"I am often asked: why does Australia, as a middle-ranking power, speak out... on matters which are more directly the business of the superpowers?... The best answer to this question would be to take the person asking it to any Australian town, from the largest to the smallest, and invite them to look at the memorial he would find there to the Australians who died in the wars of this century. The lists are long. Too many Australians have died in places remote from their homes... for us to be unconcerned about the preservation of world peace.

(Speech to the Zionist Council of Victoria, 3 May, 1981, p 27)

Retrospectivity and 'Bottom of the Harbour' Tax Schemes

"I can understand opposition to retrospectivity as a principle and... I certainly share that view.... (But) you have got the principle of retrospectivity standing against the principle of fairness, and the Government is determined that the principle of fairness must be given priority in this instance.... Nobody should be expected to pay more tax than they need to. Nobody should be expected to forego the reasonable use of the legally allowable deductions, but there is a big difference between this and the pursuit of blatant and artificial schemes which result in contrived reduction from tax, evasion from tax, or breaking of laws..."

(Liberal Party Breakfast, Brisbane, 7 October 1982, pp 182-83)

Timeline of the Life of
The Rt Hon Malcolm Fraser, AC, CH, PC

Life: 21 May 1930 – 20 March 2015

Member for Wannon: 10 December 1955 – 31 March 1983

Prime Minister of Australia: 11 November 1975 – 11 March 1983. At that time, Fraser was Australia's second longest serving Prime Minister.

Early life and early politics

21 May 1930: Fraser was born in Toorak, Melbourne, the son of Mr J Neville Fraser, a World War I veteran educated at Melbourne University and Magdalen College, Oxford, and Mrs Una Fraser (nee Woolf), who grew up in Perth, and excelled in the Arts. Fraser was the Grandson of Senator Sir Simon Fraser, who was a member of the Victorian and Commonwealth Parliaments, a member of the Conventions which framed the Australian Constitution, and the discoverer of artesian water in Queensland.

1940-1943: Fraser boarded at Tudor House, a small Anglican school in regionalNew South Wales.

1944-1948: Fraser was a day boy at Melbourne Grammar School.

1949-1952: Fraser enrolled at Magdalen College, Oxford, where he read Modern Greats (Philosophy, Politics and Economics). He later remarked that Oxford had taught him how to think. He became an Honorary Fellow of Magdalen College in 1982.

1952: Fraser returned to Australia, where he lived and worked at the family property *Nareen*, at Nareen in Western Victoria.

November 1953: Fraser won preselection for the Federal Electorate of Wannon in Western Victoria. He ran on a platform of social reform without the nationalisation he had seen in England.

January 1954: Fraser, as a candidate, began delivering weekly radio broadcasts titled *One Australia* to the Wannon electorate. These 'electorate talks' on Sunday evenings continued throughout his parliamentary career, including his Prime Ministership, when they were often 'agenda setters' for the forthcoming week.

May 1954: Fraser lost to the sitting Labor member for Wannon by 17 votes in the 1954 election. He subsequently became the Liberal candidate for the next election.

Private Member (Backbencher) 1955 - 1966

10 December 1955: Fraser won Wannon easily in the 1955 election. At age 25, he was the youngest Member of the Federal Parliament.

22 February 1956: Fraser gave his maiden speech in Parliament.

9 December 1956: Fraser was married to Miss Tamara (Tamie) Beggs, daughter of Mr and Mrs S. R. Beggs of Nareeb Nareeb, Glenthompson, in Western Victoria. The Frasers had four children—Mark, Angela, Hugh and Phoebe.

1957: Fraser gave his first major speech in Parliament, in which he spoke in support of the Free Trade Agreement with Japan.

1959: Fraser's abhorrence of racism begins appearing on the public record.

1961: Peter Nixon became the Member for the electorate of Gippsland

1962: The Menzies Government *Commonwealth Electoral Act* was enacted, which provided that all indigenous Australians have the right to enrol and vote at federal elections.

1964: Fraser spent two months in Washington D.C., with a *Leader Grant* from the US Department of State. Fraser saw the challenges of the Vietnam War from inside the US Government. Whitlam was on the same program.

26 January 1966: Sir Robert Menzies retired after his record term as Prime Minister.

26 January, 1966: Harold Holt succeeded Menzies as Prime Minister.

Minister and Cabinet Minister, 1966-1972

January 1966: Fraser was appointed to Holt's ministry as Minister for the Army. Australia had troops fighting in the Vietnam War.

17 December 1967: Prime Minister Holt disappeared in the surf at Portsea.

December 1967: John McEwen became interim Prime Minister.

December 1967: John Gorton became Leader of the

Parliamentary Liberal Party and Prime Minister.

February 1968: Fraser was appointed Minister for Education and Science, a Cabinet position, in the Gorton ministry.

c. September 1969: Fraser used the word 'multicultural' – which was not in common use at that time - in an important speech. He argued that love of and loyalty to Australia were in no way incompatible with differences in culture and affection for a person's homeland.

12 November 1969: Fraser was promoted to become Minister for Defence at the height of the Vietnam War and at a time of growing opposition to the war.

2 February 1971: Doug Anthony became Leader of the Country Party.

9 March 1971: Fraser resigned as Minister for Defence.

10 March 1971: Gorton resigned as Prime Minister.

10 March 1971: William McMahon became Prime Minister.

20 July 1971: Fraser delivered his wide-ranging Deakin Lecture at The University of Melbourne.

20 August 1971: Fraser was appointed Minister for Education and Science in the McMahon ministry.

2 December 1972: The Liberal-Country Party Coalition Government was defeated in the Federal election after 23 years in office.

December 1972: The Australian Labor Party took Government with Whitlam as Prime Minister.

Opposition 1972 - 1975

December 1972: Billy Snedden became Leader of the Liberal Party and Leader of the Opposition.

December 1972: Fraser was appointed Shadow Minister for Primary Industry.

August 1973: Fraser became Shadow Minister for Industrial Relations in a Shadow Ministry reshuffle.

11 April 1974: Whitlam announced snap double dissolution election.

18 May 1974: The ALP retained government in the election with a reduced majority in the House of Representatives.

26 November 1974: Fraser unsuccessfully challenged Snedden for leadership of the Liberal Party.

13 December 1974: Rex Connor, Minister for Minerals and Energy, was authorised to pursue a large Middle East loan through Tirath Khemlani.

24-25 December 1974: Cyclone Tracy destroyed Darwin.

5 January 1975: The Tasman Bridge in Hobart collapsed after being hit by a ship.

9 February 1975: Labor Senator Lionel Murphy resigned to join the High Court, and was replaced by Cleaver Bunton who sat as an independent.

21 March 1975: Fraser successfully challenged Snedden and became Leader of the Opposition and Leader of the Liberal Party at the age of 45.

Leader of the Opposition - 1975

c. 21 March 1975: Fraser made a statement to downplay speculation about the issue of supply.

Mid 1975: There was discord between Fraser and Whitlam as Fraser criticised Whitlam's refusal to admit refugees from Vietnam.

2 June 1975: Lance Barnard, the ALP Member for Bass and former Deputy Leader of the Parliamentary Labor Party, resigned from Parliament.

28 June 1975: Liberal candidate Kevin Newman won the Bass by-election with a 17.5% swing against Labor.

30 June 1975: Labor Senator Bernie Millner (Qld) died, and was replaced by Albert Field.

2 July 1975: Whitlam dismissed Jim Cairns – formerly the Treasurer but at the time Minister for the Environment – from the Ministry for misleading parliament over the 'Loans Affair'.

14 October 1975: Whitlam dismissed Rex Connor, the Minister for Minerals and Energy, from the Ministry for misleading parliament over the 'Loans Affair'.

15 October 1975: Fraser announced the Opposition would block supply.

16 October 1975: The Senate blocked the Government's supply bills.

16 October – 8 November 1975: Parliament debated the constitutional situation. Governor-General Sir John Kerr had some discussions with both Whitlam and Fraser.

3 November 1975: Fraser made an offer to Whitlam to pass

the Supply Bills if an election was called by May 1976. Whitlam declined the offer.

11 November 1975: The Governor-General dismissed Prime Minister Whitlam.

11 November 1975: Fraser became the 22nd Prime Minister of Australia in a caretaker role and a double dissolution election was called.

11 November 1975: First Fraser Government ministry commenced.

Prime Minister

13 December 1975: Fraser and the Coalition won government in the federal election, securing a 55-seat majority.

22 December 1975: Second Fraser Government ministry commenced.

1 June 1976: Fraser delivered his 'State of the World' speech, introducing his new era in Australian foreign policy.

1976: Fraser's first overseas visits as Prime Minister were to China and Japan.

16 June 1976: The Australia-Japan Treaty of Friendship was signed, just over thirty years since the Japanese surrender in World War II.

27-30 July 1976: Fraser visited Washington, New York and Boston. Endowed a Chair in Australian Studies at Harvard University.

17 August 1976: Treasurer Philip Lynch presented the Budget. Nobody said the Government should have cut harder.

22 September 1976: Fraser spoke at the Canberra Times 50th anniversary.

27 September 1976: Fraser delivered Roy Milne Memorial Lecture in Sydney.

1976: Northern Territory was granted self-government and the Aboriginal Land Rights (Northern Territory) Act was enacted, a significant political achievement for Fraser and for the nation.

October 1976: Fraser made a State visit to Jakarta for discussions with President Suharto.

27 October 1976: Fraser addressed the Hobart Press Club.

18 November 1976: The Commonwealth Treasury was split into two separate departments: Treasury, and Finance.

28 November 1976: The Treasurer announced a 17.5% devaluation of the Australian dollar, and a 'managed float'.

December 1976: Aboriginal Land Rights (Northern Territory) Act became law.

7-30 March 1977: Queen Elizabeth II and the Duke of Edinburgh visited Australia.

9 March 1977: Fraser spoke at the opening of the Genesis of a Gallery exhibition in Canberra.

17 March 1977: Green Paper on Population and Immigration tabled, proposing increased immigration.

June 1977: Commonwealth Heads of Government Meeting in London, at which Fraser took a leading role in supporting sporting boycotts against South Africa. The Commonwealth countries signed the Gleneagles Agreement, which affirmed opposition to racial discrimination in sport and insisted that

South Africa abolish apartheid.

21-23 June 1977: Fraser visited Washington and New York.

1977: The Monetary Policy Committee, a Standing Committee of Cabinet, was established. This committee took most key economic decisions - including establishing the Campbell Committee Review of the Australian Financial System (appointed January 1978) - laying much of the groundwork for the later Hawke and Keating economic reforms.

10 December 1977: In a general election for the House of Representatives and for 34 (out of 64) Senate seats, Fraser won re-election in another significant victory. As in 1975, the Liberals won enough seats to govern without the Country Party, however Fraser retained the Coalition. Fraser appointed John Howard as Treasurer after only three years in Parliament.

20 December 1977: Third Fraser Government Ministry commenced.

1 January 1978: Recognising the importance of a voice for multiculturalism in Australia, Fraser created the Special Broadcasting Service (SBS) to provide multilingual and multicultural television services.

30 March 1978: Fraser delivered the Inaugural Sir Robert Menzies Lecture at Monash University.

3 April 1978: Fraser spoke at National Aboriginal Conference in Canberra.

May 1978: Fraser presented Report of Galbally Review of Post-Arrival Programs and Services to Cabinet - all 57 recommendations were adopted.

1978: Construction of the new Parliament House approved.

1978: Tamie and Malcolm Fraser toured Aboriginal communities in Arnhem Land and Alice Springs to address the issues with policy making that was falling far short of improving the social, economic, and health outcomes for Indigenous communities. Throughout his time in government, Fraser's bipartisan Aboriginal policies centred on his deep respect for human rights and self-determination.

31 October 1978: Fraser addressed the Australian Academy of Technological Sciences in Canberra.

1-3 January 1979: Fraser visited Washington for discussions with President Carter.

1979: The Australian Refugee Advisory Council was created for the settlement of refugees, particularly from Asia. Fraser's compassionate approach to refugee settlement was the tangible mark of the end to White Australia. The Fraser Government accepted significant numbers of refugees from Lebanon and East Timor.

1-2 August 1979: Commonwealth Heads of Government meeting in Lusaka - Fraser pushed for support for majority rule in Rhodesia.

1980: Fraser pressured the Australian Olympic Committee to boycott the 1980 Moscow Olympic Games because of the Soviet invasion of Afghanistan.

31 January - 7 February 1980: Fraser visited Washington for discussions with President Carter en route to Europe, where he held discussions with the Prime Minister of the UK, the President of France and the Chancellor of Germany - after which, at the suggestion of the two European leaders, he returned to report to President Carter on his discussions with them.

3 March 1980: Fraser opened National Aboriginal Employment Development Committee campaign in Sydney.

6 March 1980: Fraser spoke at Launch of the World Conservation Strategy.

26 May 1980: High Court of Australia building in Canberra opened by the Queen.

1 August 1979: Commonwealth Heads of Government meeting in Lusaka—Fraser pushed for support for majority rule in Rhodesia.

10 September 1980: Costigan Royal Commission into the Painters and Dockers Union appointed.

18 October 1980: Fraser Government returned in the Federal election with a 21 seat majority in the House of Representatives, while losing control of the Senate.

26 January 1981: Fraser opened Australian Institute of Sport in Canberra.

23 March 1981: Fraser opened Congress of the International Booksellers Federation in Melbourne.

14 April 1981: Human Rights Commission Act enacted.

30 April 1981: Review of Commonwealth Functions (Razor Gang) Report handed down.

1981: In an anti-apartheid stance, Fraser stopped the Springbok rugby team from entering Australia.

June 1981: Fraser visited Mexico for discussions including upcoming Cancun meeting.

29 June – 1July 1981: Fraser visited Washington and New York. On 30 June President Ronald Reagan hosted a State

Dinner for Fraser at the White House. Subsequent to this visit, Fraser visited Ottowa for discussions with Prime Minister Trudeau.

29 July 1981: Fraser attended wedding of Prince Charles and Princess Diana in London during significant industrial unrest in Australia. Fraser met with several world leaders during this visit, including an informal meeting with President Sadat of Egypt.

7 August 1981: Fraser addressed the inaugural meeting of the Policy Assembly of the Victorian Liberal Party.

26 October 1981: Fraser opened the World Heritage Committee Meeting in Sydney.

16 November 1981: Fraser presented the Businesswoman of the Year Award in Sydney.

30 November 1981: Fraser delivered Inaugural Address to the Institute of Multicultural Affairs.

10 December 1981: Fraser inaugurated Human Rights Commission.

8 April 1982: Fraser defeated Andrew Peacock 54/27 in a leadership spill.

7 May 1982: Fifth Fraser Government ministry commenced, due to reshuffle.

16-17 May 1982: Fraser visited Washington, where he had discussions with President Reagan. He went on to visit Canada and Japan, for discussions with their respective Prime Ministers.

1 – 10 August 1982: Fraser made an official visit to China, during which he met with Paramount Leader Deng Xiao Peng

and other Chinese leaders. During this mission, Fraser also visited the Philippines to meet President Marcos, Malaysia to meet Prime Minister Dr Mahathir, and New Zealand to attend the South Pacific Forum.

12 October 1982: National Gallery of Australia in Canberra opened by the Queen.

3 February 1983: Fraser announced a double dissolution.

3 February, 1983: Bob Hawke became Parliamentary Leader of the ALP, and Leader of the Opposition.

5 March 1983: Coalition defeated in the election in a 24-seat swing. Fraser resigned as Liberal leader. Hawke became Prime Minister.

11 March 1983: Fraser officially resigned prime ministership.

31 March 1983: Fraser retired from Parliament at age fifty-two.

Post-Parliament

1985-86: Fraser served as Co-Chairman of the Commonwealth Group of Eminent Persons on South Africa to end apartheid. In November 1985, he addressed the United Nations General Assembly asserting the duty of nations to take a firmer stance against apartheid. Fraser spent time at Harvard and in Washington DC lobbying Congress and President Reagan.

1987: Fraser founded the Australian branch of CARE, a foreign aid organisation. He remained chair until 2002. During this period, from 1990 to 1995, he served as the President of CARE International. The organisation, which provides humanitarian aid in times of crisis, was faced with significant emergencies during Fraser's time as part of the leadership, including crises in Bangladesh, Sudan, Somalia, Rwanda, Bosnia and Kosovo.

1988: Fraser was awarded the AC (Companion of the Order of Australia).

1989-90: Fraser served as Chairman of the UN-Secretary General's Expert Group on African Commodity Issues.

1984-1986: Fraser was appointed a distinguished international fellow at the American Enterprise Institute.

1984: Fraser joined - and subsequently became Chairman of - the *Interaction Council*, a private international group of former heads of governments founded in 1983 by Takeo Fukuda of Japan. Among other projects, Fraser helped in the Council's attempt to draft a *Universal Declaration of Responsibilities*.

1985: Fraser was appointed a Fellow of the Centre for International Affairs at Harvard University.

2000: Fraser was awarded the Human Rights Medal by the Australian Human Rights Commission.

2002: Fraser published *Common Ground – Issues that should bind and not divide us*, comprising eight essays on economic, global, and humanitarian concerns.

2007: Fraser was appointed Professorial Fellow at the Asia Pacific Centre for Military Law within the University of Melbourne.

2010: Fraser resigned from the Liberal Party.

2010: Fraser (with Margaret Simons) published *Malcolm Fraser: The Political Memoirs*.

2014: Fraser (with Cain Roberts) published *Dangerous Allies*.

Malcolm Fraser died at the Epworth Hospital in Richmond, Victoria, in March 2015. A State Funeral was held at Scots Church in Melbourne. His resting place is in the Prime Ministers Memorial Garden at the Melbourne General Cemetery.

Select Bibliography

Ayres, Philip, *Malcolm Fraser A Biography*, Heinemann, Richmond, 1987

Campbell Committee, *Australian Financial System – Final Report of the Committee of Inquiry*, AGPS, Canberra, 1981

"F, R.K", (Roy Forward), 'Australian Political Chronicle', in *The Australian Journal of Politics and History*, Vols. 21 & 22, 1975 & 1976

Fraser, Malcolm, *Common Ground – Issues that should Bind and not Divide Us*, Penguin, Australia, 2002

Fraser, Malcolm, and Simons, Margaret, *Malcolm Fraser The Political Memoirs*, The Meigunyah Press - MUP, Melbourne, 2010

Fraser, Malcolm, with Cain Roberts, *Dangerous Allies*, MUP, Melbourne, 2014

Grattan, Michelle, (Ed), *Australian Prime Ministers*, New Holland Publishers, Sydney, 2000

Gregory, Alan, (Ed), *The Menzies Lectures 1978-1998*, The Sir Robert Menzies Lecture Trust, Melbourne, 1999

Henderson, Gerard, *Menzies Child, The Liberal Party of Australia*, Harper Collins, Pymble, rev. ed. 1998

Kemp, D.A., 'Advisers and Decisions 1976.' *Australian Journal of Public Administration*, Vol. 66(1), March 2007

Kemp, David, 'Leadership Practices: Reflections on Australian Political Leadership' in Paul 't Hart, David Uhr, *Public Leadership:Perspectives and Practices*, Canberra, Australian National University, E Press, 2008

Martin (Vic Martin) Committee, *Review of the Australian Financial System*, AGPS, Canberra, 1984

Puplick, C.J., and Southey, R.J., *Liberal Thinking*, Macmillan, South Melbourne, 1980

Rhodes, R.A.W., and Tiernan, Anne, *The Gate Keepers: Lessons from Prime Ministers' Chiefs of Staff*, Melbourne University Press, Melbourne, 2014

Ryle, Gilbert, *The Concept of Mind*, Hutchinson, Great Britain, 1949

Starr, Graham, *The Liberal Party of Australia: A Documentary History*, Drummond Heinemann, Richmond Vic, 1980

Tiver, Peter, *The Liberal Party: Principles and Performance*, Jacaranda Press, Milton Queensland, 1978

Wanna, John, et al, *Managing Public Expenditure in Australia*, Allen and Unwin, Australia, 2000

Weller, Patrick, *Malcolm Fraser PM: A Study in Prime Ministerial Power in Australia*, Penguin, Ringwood, 1989

White, D.M,, *The Philosophy of the Australian Liberal Party*, Hutchinson, Melbourne, 1978

White, D.M. and Kemp, D.A. (eds), *Malcolm Fraser on Australia*, Hill of Content, Australia, 1986

White, Denis, *The World of Man*, The Create Space Independent Publishing Platform, South Carolina, 2013

White, D.M., 'Political Communication and Democratic Government' in *Politics*, Vol 24 (1), 1989

White, D.M., 'Backup for Ministers' in *Politics*, Vol 23 (1), 1988

White, D.M., 'Constitutionalism', in *Politics*, Vol 16 (2), 1981

White, D.M., 'Power and Liberty', in *Political Studies*, Vol 19 (1), 1971

White, D.M., 'Prolegomena to the Study of Democracy', in *The Australian Journal of Politics and History*, Vol 18 (2), 1972

White, D.M., 'Negative Liberty', in *Ethics*, Vol 80 (3), 1970, Univ of Chicago Press, Chicago